Father To Son

by Patrick C. Burke

Son To Father

© 2019 Patrick C. Burke. All rights reserved.

Printed in the United States of America.
ISBN: 978-0-578-62168-5
1st Edition.

No part of this book may be used or reproduced
without the written permission of the copyright holders.

Cover illustration:
Stefan Tur / stefantur@usa.com

Cover and interior design:
Kathryn D'Amanda—MillRace Design / kda@mill-race.com

Copy editor:
Bob Cronin

Every reasonable effort has been made to identify owners of copyright.
Errors or omissions will be corrected in subsequent editions.

Dedicated to

to my father Albert

and my son Adrian

Introduction

My son, Adrian, and I have a long tradition of exchanging letters every Christmas morning. Over the last twenty years the letters reflect the maturity of a small boy into a well-adjusted young man. This journey of self-discovery proved to build and fortify our unique father son relationship. This tradition served to allow Adrian to grow spiritually and emotionally and learned to express his deepest feelings. My letters to Adrian gave me the opportunity to express ideas that I believed to be important as he develops his character.

This short book captures the essence of the growth of our relationship and brief stories to emphasis a point of character development. My intention in writing the book is to assist others in developing deep and healthy relationships with young people. I hope you enjoy it and find it useful.

P.B.

"We have great hope for your future and believe that when you put forth the effort, you can achieve your dreams."

—Dad, Christmas 2003

Commitment Rewarded

I started bringing my son to work when he was only a few weeks old. On Saturday mornings, he would be in his portable car seat on my desk. As he grew, I would spend time with him explaining how business works in considerable detail. Today, as an adult, he frequently talks with me about his business career. When asked, I share my entrepreneurial insights.

After he applied with his employer, we discussed his upcoming interview. He was well prepared after fully researching the firm, including its history, product offering and the clients it served, as well as the competitive landscape. As we discussed interview questions, I said there was one that he would likely be asked and that he needed to be prepared to answer it in a way that comes from the heart. The question: "Why do you want this job?" Before you provide the answer, I told him, you will need to gently and tactfully explain to the questioner that you are not there for a job but rather a career, articulating your commitment to the organization if hired.

While in sales support, he immersed himself in self-learning on how the organization's successful sales enterprise operated and traits of the best salespeople. After a year, we had a discussion on how to approach the possibility of moving into a salesman's role; I'm a salesman and have tremendous respect for committed and successful professional salespeople. I said that if he was committed to doing it, he should make the organization aware of this and ask what he needed to do to be considered for the position. The organization provided him the guidance he requested, and he went to work broadening and strengthening his knowledge of professional sales skills.

In time, he was asked to move into the role of account executive, directly responsible for sales from existing and new clients. As he submitted the paperwork, he reiterated his appreciation for the opportunity and his continued commitment to the success of the business. Now he is focused on becoming the best account executive he can be.

I tell you this tale as a proud father and as a business owner who recognizes the power of commitment at every stage of a business career. Lukewarmness can stymie the most promising opportunities.

So let's get to work.

"I was comfortable going to school in Buffalo, as I had a lot of friends and the environment was similar to that of my high school. But I wanted more."
— Adrian, Christmas 2011 (19)

The Rule of Motion

A longtime friend asked what the most important thing I've learned in business is. I said it's the importance of the mindset captured in the command, "Keep moving." My friend followed up with a quizzical "Why?"

That sentence can mean keep growing, keep learning, keep looking for life experiences that will build your character and enhance your relationships with others.

The rewards in life come from the relationships we develop in our personal lives as well as in our business or public lives. In my experience, it's well worth the effort to take the initiative. Reach out. Connect with and assist others without an expectation of reciprocity. It becomes the crucible in which we build character.

Character—who you are as a person—will take you further than anything you learn in a classroom.

It turns out that some of the most valuable lessons are not the lessons that we are taught in school. They are the lessons we learn from life. It's only from experience in living that we develop character. To achieve excellence in being is far more important than excellence in merely achieving.

It is all ignited by the words, "Keep moving." That can mean favoring action over inaction, favoring involvement and engagement over hanging back and looking for reasons to take it easy.

Wherever your path leads, I would urge you to become involved in the life of your communities, whether it's at home or work. Wherever you are, be a contributor. Our communities, our churches and our schools need people who are active and involved. Or as my dad used to say, "You can't stand in front of the stove of life and expect heat if you don't throw in some wood once in a while."

Keep moving.

Those words can remind us that we need to continually challenge ourselves. Learning never stops.

I encourage you to work on the hard things. Challenge yourself. The rewards and personal satisfaction are much greater when you attempt the difficult task, rather than seeking the path of least resistance.

Don't spend too much time worrying about failure. You will experience it. The only alternative—the only way to not fail—is to not try at all. So don't be afraid of failing. Be afraid of not trying.

I've always been willing to try new things. And I've learned much more from my mistakes than I have from my successes.

Remember, failure is an event—it's not a person. I've found that intelligent perseverance carries the day. Make a plan and stick to it. But do it intelligently. Sometimes you'll find you've made a wrong choice. There's no shame in that, as long as you have what it takes to admit a mistake and change.

So if there's nothing else you remember from this column, remember these two words: Keep moving.

> "I strive toward success with the love and support from people who believe in me."
> —Adrian, Christmas 2015 (23)

The Person Behind the Pitch

Lou Izzo, known as "the pitching guy," died August 9, 2016. He got the moniker from his work with aspiring young ballplayers, particularly pitchers. To remember him in this way is wonderful but doesn't do justice to the larger impact he had on so many, including me.

I met Lou following my graduation from Cornell. Lou was a sales manager and trainer for Aetna and was charged with making me a productive businessman. His training techniques were unique; where others relied on highly structured and scripted approaches to make the sale, Lou would say first we establish a relationship and then maybe we make a sale.

He started with the basics, making sure I referred to people by their name, saying there is not a sweeter sound than hearing your name. He went on to tell me that the importance of good manners and "please" and "thank you" is not optional but a requirement in our business vocabulary. He taught me how to properly greet people in a business setting—shaking hands, making proper eye contact and acknowledging everyone in the room no matter their position. Lou would tell me that before you can sell something to somebody, you need to get to know them. Where others were stressing the importance of memorizing a sales script, Lou was teaching me how to start and develop a productive conversation that would lead to a much deeper understanding and appreciation of the prospective customer.

Most of what Lou taught didn't come naturally, as I was a bit shy and intimidated. Lou's solution was, "Practice, practice, practice." Where others taught the importance of selling features of the product, Lou would say, "You are the product." I was lucky to have him as my teacher and mentor, and our relationship stayed intact until he took his last breath.

My story is one of hundreds that could be told about Lou Izzo. I found it rare in business to have someone commit so completely to your success that their success wasn't even part of the equation. Lou was a great teacher, coach, teammate and cheerleader, but most of all he was a great friend to many.

When legendary investor Warren Buffett was asked how wealth should be measured, he responded by saying that real wealth is counted by the number of loving friends you have at your death. By that measure, Lou Izzo died a very wealthy man.

Bidding you a fine adieu, sweet Lou.

> "It's important that your curiosity is a thirst that can't be quenched."
> —Dad, Christmas 2014

Creative Solutions

A friend asked me what I thought was the reason some companies grow to a certain size and can't seem to grow any further. I said it could be a number of reasons. I could tell he wasn't satisfied with that answer by his body language, which said, "You can do better than that."

He said, "Do you think people lose their drive and become a bit lazy?" I said I think that is an easy explanation, but likely not correct. He followed up with, maybe their service or product is outdated, and there are limited growth opportunities? Again, I responded, possibly, but unlikely. At this point he got a bit frustrated with me and said, OK, it's your turn, and no generalizations.

I said one thing I've observed in growing companies that is lacking in companies whose growth has plateaued is what I refer to as the "competency brownout." I could tell from the puzzled look on my friend's face that an explanation was in order, so I went further in explaining myself.

We think of competence as having the knowledge, skill and ability to do a particular job, and of course that is true. A competency brownout occurs when an organization has these abilities but lacks two vital traits you see in growing companies: curiosity and creativity.

Curiosity and creativity are the headwaters of all growth, and without them the business growth will run dry. I've seen it time and time again—good, smart people spending their days perfecting the obsolete, because it is what they know and is generally the safest path. They are unlikely to change and beget a slow death of the business.

Curiosity and creativity are best developed by listening to your clients and prospects to learn the obstacles they are facing and how you may come up with a creative solution. A creative solution is always straightforward and should be easily and logically communicated to your prospect or customer, and its significant value should be self-evident.

Avoiding a competency brownout also requires a tireless commitment to learn everything you can about what is going on in your industry; in other words, you need a high curiosity quotient. In your search for meaning, you will need to find the fulcrum by which your new idea or next generation product will be delivered into a marketplace that is yet unaware of its need.

Curiosity and creativity are two traits that are requirements for any organization that wants to grow. A friend of mind once told me that if all you have is a hammer, every problem looks like a nail.

So let's get to work.

> "I'm pleased that you are developing an appreciation for theology, philosophy, theater and Latin. They will serve you well in the development of ideas and appreciation for others."
> —Dad, Christmas 2011

Timeless Wisdom

I received an email from a purchaser of my book, Outside Insights, wondering what other inspirational books I would recommend for her daughter who recently graduated from college. If you are a frequent reader of this column, you may have come to appreciate that I'm not a big fan of the modern-day, self-help gurus, complete with their image consultants and branding agents, but prefer more of the classic writers and philosophers, sprinkled in with entrepreneurs.

I emailed her a couple of ideas that have helped me maintain focus throughout my business career, though I continue to learn something new almost every day. The first was written by entrepreneur and department store magnate Marshall Field in the second half of the 19th century, Twelve Things to Remember:

1. The value of time.
2. The success of perseverance.
3. The pleasure of working.
4. The dignity of simplicity.
5. The worth of character.
6. The power of kindness.
7. The influence of example.
8. The obligations of duty.
9. The wisdom of economy.
10. The virtue of patience.
11. The improvement of talent.
12. The joy of originating.

Another favorite author of mine is Elbert Hubbard from East Aurora, New York, who started as a traveling salesman for the Buffalo-based Larkin Soap Co. in the late 19th century before he became an influential writer, artist and philosopher. Unfortunately, he died much too early, at the age of 58, on May 7, 1915, as a passenger on the RMS Lusitania that was torpedoed and sunk by a German submarine 11 miles off the coast of Ireland, at a place called Old Head. I visited the commemorative memorial plaque, with my son and brother-in-law, in June 2014.

Hubbard's essay A Message to Garcia laments the difficulty in finding employees who are self-reliant, industrious, intelligent and reliable. After the essay was published in 1899, it was made into a pamphlet, and it is estimated that over 40 million have been printed. In the essay, Hubbard writes: "It is not book-learning young men need, nor instruction about this or that, but a stiffening of the vertebrae which will cause them to be loyal to a trust, to act promptly, concentrate their energies; do the thing—'carry a message to Garcia!'"

Elbert Hubbard's Scrap Book, published in 1923, is a wonderful collection of essays, opinions, and quotations that he collected throughout his life about success, humanity, nature, love and war from some of the great thinkers, writers and statesman throughout history. I can assure you a thought-provoking journey through time.

So let's get to work.

"I remember riding in the car as a young boy with you listening to Zig Ziglar and his many stories. At the time, I did not think he had the most entertaining content for a long car ride, but now coincidentally find myself listening to those same types of programs."
—Adrian, Christmas 2018 (26)

The Power of Storytelling

I was at a meeting recently with several business associates where we were talking about the power of effective communication. The conversation quickly turned to a 35-page PowerPoint presentation one of the participants handed out. I attend a lot of meetings and have determined PowerPoint seems to be the drug of choice to anesthetize and sterilize your intended target—your audience.

I asked the group if someone could tell me a story of what is in the PowerPoint presentation without opening it up. They looked at me as if to say, "The presentation is the story," but were too kind to say that and asked what I meant. I said a simple narrative on why I should spend valuable time sitting through a 35-page PowerPoint is all I'm asking.

My point being that the art of storytelling has been usurped by lifeless software. Storytelling is an essential component of effective persuasion. It's important to note that persuasion is when you convince someone to take action for their benefit; manipulation is when you convince them to take action for your benefit.

Good storytellers recognize that words have shapes, colors and effervescent. Storytellers work tirelessly to determine and use the precise word and combination of words to paint a picture of their idea in the mind of the other person. Words are their precious commodity, and the wasting of even one of them is troubling and could introduce the risk of your point being covered over by the smoldering ashes of confusion. Good storytellers appreciate that tone, pitch and speed create the vehicle by which their story will be transported. Finally, good storytellers know when to stop talking and end with a point of emphasis.

Before you delve into your next PowerPoint deck and limit your storytelling to slide reading, take the time to convert your thoughts into an interesting and persuasive story on why your audience should be interested in your presentation. Don't get frustrated if you are struggling putting the words together; it will take time and a lot of practice. Once you get it down, your effectiveness will rise significantly.

Paul Harvey, the late radio personality, reportedly said that once you have a good story, don't change it; rather, change the audience. Sounds like common sense to me.

So let's get to work.

> "Fordham had a significant impact on the makeup of your personality, giving you a comfortable though respectful nature when interacting with others."
> —Dad, Christmas 2014

Dressed to Reflect

I received a flattering email from a devoted reader who asked my advice on guiding her son, who recently accepted a job with a large professional service firm, on how he should build an appropriate work wardrobe. I receive quite a few emails, but this one caught my attention, and I inquired why she was seeking my advice. She told me she raised her son alone after her husband tragically passed away when the boy was young, and after reading my column the past few years, hoped I'd have some thoughts on the topic. The following is what I told her.

First, you need to determine what kind of professional impression you want to leave with people you are meeting or working with. Your attire should reflect respect for those around you and display a particular attention to detail consistent with the thoroughness of your work ethic. A mentor of mine once told me to remember "manners count, and the clothes make the man." As a young professional, my father would tell me a well-dressed executive brings a subtle confident presence to every meeting.

I've found that style of clothing is individually determined and should reflect your attitude and personality. A good haberdasher can provide useful guidance in building your wardrobe. Upon getting to know you, they can make specific clothing recommendations to reflect your personality. Additionally, the fit of the garment is more important than the material. The late Peter DiGiorgio, who was a Master Tailor, told me that a well-fitting inexpensive suit is better than an ill-fitting expensive one. I've found his advice invaluable. Your professional attire is an investment in your career and should be acquired and suitably maintained over a period of years.

In 1987, I was working in New York City and was preparing for a meeting with a prospective client. I was 26, and a senior partner of the firm called me to his office. He asked me if I thought we would get the business. I said yes. He inquired why, and I went on to explain that I thought we had a service offering superior to our competition's. He then said something I'll never forget: "If you are selling a superior product, shouldn't you look like one?"

So let's get to work.

> "A thorough examination of your own conscience from time to time is always a worthwhile endeavor to ensure your own actions are consistent with your faith and beliefs."
> — Dad, Christmas 2006

The Demands of Justice

On a few occasions, I've been asked how one's faith enters into the world of business. I'm reluctant to offer opinions on matters of faith and its relationship to business. It seems strange that violence should ever attend religion, yet history tells us this has been a perennial problem throughout the ages.

I've learned in business that it's more important to search and find common ground, without consideration of faith.

The traditions of my Christian faith were born out of the amalgamation of faith and reason, between Jewish and Greek philosophers. We Catholics refer to this as the "logos."

In business and non-business situations, it requires a person to recognize the "wedding" between the heart and the mind. Our feeling and our thinking must support each other in order to gain peace and understanding.

As Americans, we recognize discrete responsibilities of government and religion, as well as the individual's natural rights within these spheres—primarily the right to seek the truth and act on conscience.

The primary job of an entrepreneur is to build a successful business, with earning a profit as its No. 1 priority and outstanding customer service its No. 1 objective. In pursuing that goal, people face choices about how they will conduct themselves ethically, morally and even spiritually.

If one accepts the premise that individual freedom comes with the obligation to do what we "ought," not just what we "want," then the responsibility of the businessperson will become an ongoing search in determining the demands of justice in the marketplace and larger community.

Negotiating the demands of justice is where the journey in the thought of the businessperson begins. Ancient Greek philosophy detailed the four secular traits of an individual's character that form the basis for, and strengthen, ethical behavior. They are known to us as the cardinal virtues: wisdom, courage, moderation and justice.

Of these, the Greeks believed wisdom to be the most important in that it is the ability to recognize, differentiate and choose between right and wrong. We think of this as reason.

In addition to Greek thought, most faiths look to a higher power as a means of perfecting their believers' minds in a way that seeks social justice.

The entrepreneur has an obligation to act on conscience for victims of social injustice and for citizens with special needs. In the end, we are all in this together.

> "I've had the privilege throughout my career to associate with many smart people and have observed that intelligence alone rarely leads to success."
> —Dad, Christmas 2013

Simplicity Rules

In the 14th century, a Franciscan friar, William of Ockham, devised a problem-solving principle that continues to hold true in business and life. The principle, known as "Ockham's razor," states that the simplest solution to a particular problem is likely the one that will work best.

As the business world becomes more complex with the introduction of the newest app or gadget, what is intended to make things easier can actually make your life more challenging. A trait I've observed in many successful businesspeople is that they all seem to have a set of overarching simple rules on how they conduct their business affairs. One friend won't pursue a project unless he identifies an alternative way out if things change and the initial opportunity goes away. Another friend has a rule to never pay more than book value for a company. Legendary investor Warren Buffett has a standing rule that the only way to make money at an auction is to not show up. Napoleon Bonaparte had a standing rule for his army: "March towards the gunfire."

In the book Simple Rules: How to Thrive in a Complex World, authors Donald Sull and Kathleen Eisenhardt explain "rules for rules" and the two basic types of rules, one for better decision-making and the other for doing things better. Good rule-makers figure out what will move the needle, identify and choose a constraint holding them back and craft the rules that address each.

Better decision-making rules fall into one of three categories: boundary, prioritization and stopping. Boundary rules help management focus when presented with many opportunities; a good boundary rule would eliminate some of the opportunities. An example would be an existing business that won't take on a new client unless it provides a minimum profitability threshold. Prioritization rules help managers rank alternatives and assign resources.

Stopping rules tell management when to reverse a decision or change course. Dan Loeb, nationally renowned investor, automatically sells any stock that drops by 10% of his purchase price.

Doing-things-better rules include how-to, coordination and timing. How-to rules provide the basics on how to execute a particular task, coordination rules speak to the organization and leadership of teams, and timing rules provide guidelines for when to take action.

The key to any rules you develop for your business or life is simplicity both in number of rules and the rules themselves. A good example is a rule for what to eat from Michael Pollen, author of The Omnivores Dilemma: "Eat food. Not too much. Mostly plants."

So let's get to work.

> "People who have recognized the need and take responsibility are rare and usually are the most successful and happy people you will meet."
> —Dad, Christmas 2005

High-Performance Models

I was asked by a friend of mine who founded and manages a large service organization when I thought an explanation becomes an excuse. After thinking about it, I answered when opportunity has been squandered. He asked me to elaborate on my answer.

Over my career I've seen poorly performing organizations that eventually go out of business, mediocre organizations that survive but don't thrive, and high-performing organizations that annually grow their revenue and profits. Poor and mediocre organizations share a common trait: They rationalize failure by accepting a well-crafted excuse made in the form of an explanation for a lost opportunity. Over time, this behavior leads to a lack of accountability for the consequence of failure.

High-performing organizations understand the anatomy of success and create an operating model that generates a cadence in which success feeds off success. High performers understand the intrinsic value of simplicity and the aim of flawless execution. My observation is that the successful business model has three components: structure, talent and accountability.

Structure involves an efficient organization that provides sales support, product delivery and customer support. It also includes a compensation structure that rewards profitable growth and encourages low performers to self-select out of the organization.

Talent starts with a rigorous and thorough hiring process. Expectations of an individual need to be crystal clear, including an understanding of what success looks like with as much specificity as possible. There needs to be an understanding on the level of support that will be available to an individual.

For high-performing organizations, accountability is a motivator, not a deterrent. Their competitive nature drives their thirst for knowing where they stand against the goal, and they work tirelessly to prove they can exceed the expectations of others. Poor and mediocre organizations cringe when held accountable for underperformance and view the exercise as punitive and unfair—ultimately deciding, consciously or subconsciously, that there is no consequence for underperformance.

This approach may appear simple, but it is not easy. It takes a significant amount of executive and leadership skill to indoctrinate an organization with a high-performance culture. It can take years to create, constant vigilance to maintain, and with poor leadership can be destroyed almost instantly.

Vince Lombardi, the legendary Green Bay Packers coach, expressed it this way: Perfection is not attainable, but if we chase perfection we can catch excellence.

So let's get to work.

"Some of my friends are Jack Wilson, David Pilkington, Ben Lovenheim, Patrick Hanna, Ben Zeiss, Tyler Reed, Brendan Glavin, Thomas Rodenhouse, Ray Kelly, and Kevin Harrington. My friends do many things for me. They cheer me up when I am sad. My friends also stand up for me."
—Adrian, Christmas 2003 (11)

Friendship at Work

On Valentine's Day, someone asked me if there was a place for friendship in business. I was curious about why she asked me the question, and she told me about a betrayal suffered at the hands of a middle manager at a large organization. I asked why the person would have done such a thing, for which she had no good answer other than that the manager was insecure and may have felt threatened by other friendships she had developed. I cautioned that friendship in the marketplace can at times be deceiving and nothing more than a wolf in sheep's clothing, or worse, a sheep in sheep's clothing.

I encouraged her to set that incident aside and said friendships in business exist, and when properly understood can lead to tremendously powerful results. Based on her experience, my answer surprised her, and she questioned what aspects of friendship I thought were important in business. To which I answered, the same ones as in life.

A friendship departs from the many acquaintances we may have in five key attributes. The first is "shared interest"; for a friendship to work, you need to be working hand in glove with your business partner. If either party treats the other as less than an equal partner, I can assure you the organization they are each charged to serve will receive less-than-optimal results.

Another aspect of friendship is to know "another self." Sometimes it is called being simpatico: We identify with the other person and want them to be successful. If done in a spirit of unity, it allows you a better understanding and self-awareness.

Our friendships must be founded on our natural, or authentic, selves. This is not to imply sameness, but rather great diversity, maintained in an environment of healthy self-esteem and acceptance. Without entering into a friendship as our natural self, the adversity that will ultimately enter into the workplace will expose the fragility of the relationship.

The last two aspects are loyalty and affection. The Marines' loyalty to the "core" and each other is captured in Semper Fidelis—always faithful, always loyal. There is a saying, "A friend walks in when the rest of the world walks out." Affection is to wish more for a friend than you do for yourself.

Friendship drives business results through excellence of intent, effort, execution and outcomes.

So let's make friends.

"I took the lessons I learned inside and outside the classroom ... into the workforce and never looked back. Countless interviews, assignments and presentations polished my professional skills and reassured the confidence I had in myself."
— Adrian, Christmas 2014 (22)

The Melding of Classroom and Boardroom

Last week, I was invited to sit in on a finals presentation of an upperclassman communication course at St. John Fisher. The course taught students advertising management and go-to-market strategy, including the process in developing and launching effective campaigns, all of which seems like a rather straightforward academic approach to learning.

What made this unique is that it didn't happen on campus.

Ferdinand and Greg Smith own Jay Advertising, a full-service advertising and branding agency they founded in Rochester in 1973. In addition to their considerable professional talents, they have a deep commitment to being meaningful contributors in supporting the quality of life we enjoy in Rochester.

Now they work with St. John Fisher on setting up a classroom inside their business, creating a unique collaboration between academia and the business world to work with students on real clients. Ferdinand, Greg and other Jay team members committed to a curriculum and "class time" of three hours a week at their studio to teach:

- Management
    - Critical pathways of communication
    - Professional writing skills
    - Budgeting
- Production and Creative
    - Brainstorming to formulate concepts
    - Brand Development and messaging
- Media
    - Optimizing their message reach using traditional channels and social networks
- Strategy/Research
    - Understanding customer behavior
    - Creating a customer journey

Three student teams, each having four to six members, were given an assignment to rebrand and launch an advertising campaign for a 12-year-old existing small business.

Typically, companies hire interns and attempt to teach them a specific aspect of their business. I have never witnessed an entire class being taught inside an active and face-paced business. I can attest after seeing the three outstanding presentations to a new learning model evolving.

The students exhibited confidence, terrific collaboration, meticulousness and the ability to defend their plan when challenged. They dressed as if in a boardroom, not a classroom. I don't know each student's name, but as a group, they made me feel good about the entrepreneurial leaders St. John Fisher is producing.

Ferdinand, Greg and the Jay team are to be congratulated for their commitment to breaking down the barriers between learning and doing and inoculating these students with the passion and drive necessary to succeed in business.

In the end, it appeared to me that these students learned a great deal and in some ways were being positively transformed in the process. These are the opportunities that can have meaningful impact over time.

So let's get to work.

> "Be a good finder in people and engage in relationships with the purpose of understanding."
> —Dad, Christmas 2012

Life in Conversation

Once in a great while I write, or say, something that moves people to take action acknowledging their agreement. It happened following my column on Memorial Day.

Emails from readers were universal in expressing their concern and discouragement at how politics has usurped the responsibility of good governance "for the people, by the people." As a businessperson, I understand competition and how the boundaries of right from wrong can become confusing in the heat of battle. We see this happening on both the national and local political scene in both parties.

Somewhere among the political posturing, we seem to have lost the art of meaningful conversation, particularly relating to sensitive topics. Several years ago, I read Fierce Conversations by Susan Scott and subsequently had a chance to meet her. In her book, she makes the case that life is one long conversation with ourselves, and when performed properly will enrich ours and the people we come in contact with immensely.

We have all seen people dump an emotionally loaded rant toward another only to hide behind the misguided belief in what they think they are entitled to, or claim it to be their authentic self. This behavior can create a repelling force in a relationship, ultimately leading to its demise. I have also observed people in business, and life, who seem to relish the role of being the "thought police" for others and never miss the opportunity to pass judgment, while not considering that silence serves as effective communication.

Scott says that until "we stop hiding behind ourselves," it's impossible to have a constructive and meaningful conversation leading to a healthy relationship. She skillfully examines and teaches how one should approach a peer, or subordinate, on a performance issue while not illuminating the emotional charge that can lead to people shutting down. Leaders understand that the conversation they are having isn't about their relationship with the other person, it is the relationship. They come prepared, understanding that words can't be unsaid and can do great harm.

Responsible leadership requires an ability to speak with "clarity, conviction and compassion" without the emotional charge associated with supremacy. Great leaders in business and politics are seekers of the truth, allowing them to assess situations, and they understand that skillful conversation is the pathway to the best outcome. I've observed far too many people spend far too much time disguising or restraining the truth, not recognizing that the truth in conversation is life's great disinfectant.

So let's get to work.

> "I've put myself in a position to succeed, and can acknowledge that, but ultimately realize I can never feel too comfortable."
> —Adrian, Christmas 2014 (22)

Two Off-Ramps to Complacency

I've written about the tradition of exchanging letters on Christmas morning with my son, Adrian. He's an adult now and has been working in Manhattan since graduating from Fordham in May 2014. In addition to chronicling the journey of a boy into manhood, common themes emerge and weave their way into each of our letters and speak to each of us in a way we both can learn. One of the themes that emerged from our Christmas 2015 letters was the destructive nature of complacency that can seep into a business career.

Adrian's insight to me was that in the marketplace, we call business having an attitude comprised of mental toughness and steely determination adorned with a profound sense of "conscious optimism" will result in achieving your greatest amount of success even when "outcomes look bleak." This inspiring idea cannot be overstated and is frequently assumed rather than taught to employees in an organization. Great attitudes alone, absent skill and experience, can rarely achieve success, while coincidently poor attitudes can ensure failure. I've seen more than a few talented businesspeople fall prey to complacency, which usually puts them on the express train to discouragement.

I mentioned to Adrian that successful organizations can also become complacent when management stops "managing" and slips into the more comfortable role of "supervising." Managers have a responsibility for an "objective," while supervisors are responsible for the completion of a "task." These are two very different roles in an organization that are frequently misunderstood.

Good managers are constantly evaluating how they may produce their product or service more efficiently, timely and effectively, while gaining an advantage over competitors in the marketplace. In order to do this effectively, they are willing to completely disband established processes and reorganize the available resources to get better and better. Leading organizations that "manage" typically exhibit a healthy amount of creative tension and a heightened sense of urgency.

Supervisors, on the other hand, focus most of their attention on the completion of a distinct set of tasks. The measure of success becomes how efficiently they complete those tasks, which is important but is not a substitute for management. Poor managers frequently misunderstand the difference and spend their time policing behaviors rather inspiring, nurturing and leading the creative process of management. Organizations that mistakenly substitute "supervising" for "managing" will ultimately become prey for a forward-thinking competitor.

In the end, our letters reinforced how important it is to continually learn from each other, and we both are better for it.

So let's get to work and continue to learn.

> "It's important to not get caught up in group thinking, but rather develop the skills to see beyond the moment to what something could become."
> —Dad, Christmas 2015

Adjust, and Quickly

On Dec. 17, 1903, Wilbur Wright's flight at Kitty Hawk stayed airborne for 59 seconds and traveled 852 feet. Ten years later, commercial aviation was born. Today, more than 3 billion people fly the friendly skies annually. The power of innovation to changes lives and how quickly it can happen are typically underestimated.

The first iPhone was introduced a dozen years ago, and today's smartphones have become an indispensable tool by which we run our lives. The smartphone is the culprit that has been at the core of turning the taxi and hotel industries worldwide on their head, through smartphone applications Uber and Airbnb. Amazon and Alibaba online innovations may put the bricks-and-mortar retailers on the endangered species lists. Google and Tesla are on a mission to send the automotive industry the way of the buggy whip makers. College professors lecture in massive open online courses, referred to as MOOC classrooms, to over 10,000 students at a time, and bank tellers are seeing fewer customers than the Maytag repairman.

This holiday season, all kinds of gadgets will be given to loved ones in a new frontier called "wearable" technology. Watches are being transformed into health regulators, personal concierge and communication devices the likes of which Maxwell Smart might have given to Agent 99. T-shirts are being imbedded with the latest physical fitness software that will allow you to measure the impact of each of your exercise regimes. Hats and shoes now provide the wearer information on calories burned, distance covered and average rate of speed. If this isn't enough, throw on a wearable camera and make a home movie to share online.

The most game-changing wearable technology is in eyewear. Eyewear is no longer just for seeing; now we can watch movies, and video games can make you an active participant. You can buy glasses that allow you to keep connected with all your other technology, unbeknownst to the person you are with.

Our world is becoming more digitized, controlled by software. Companies that don't re-create their offerings in recognition of this change are vulnerable to being dislocated and ending up in the ash heap of failed enterprises. Winning organizations will understand the rapid acceleration of technology that's disrupting business as we knew it and demonstrate the agility and creativity to adjust.

All this being said, it's OK to be nostalgic in reflecting on the past. When Neil Armstrong walked on the moon, on July 20, 1969, only 66 years after Wilbur Wright's first flight, he carried in his pocket a piece of the muslin that covered Wilbur's "Flyer 1" wings.

So let's get to work.

> "When we are in Ireland and are able to speak with the people, their caring nature is apparent, thus it is important to help them just as they help us."
> —Adrian, Christmas 2012 (20)

The Folly of Cold Persuasion

Last week I was traveling with a couple of business associates, and one asked me what I thought was the most detrimental unintended consequence of technology in business today. The question stumped me, as in a broad sense, technology that was intended to enhance communication has in many ways debased it. Well, that wasn't good enough, and my colleague leaned on me for a more precise answer.

After giving the question a bit more thought, I said PowerPoint has been the single biggest culprit in dumbing down the marketplace conversation, particularly in the use of "persuasion" in most decision-making processes. My answer was met with a fair amount of skepticism and disbelief, so I offered the following explanation.

For decades, neuroscientists have proven that for people to act, they first must care. For someone to care, there must be an "emotional component" in the decision for an individual to change from the status quo. Simply put, people buy in on emotion and justify with logic.

PowerPoint presentations have turned many sales and internal decision-making meetings into a facts-and-figures exercise complete with some of the world's best slide readers. What has been lost is the importance of developing the ability of storytelling. Scientists have also proven that storytelling, where facts are wrapped in context and delivered with emotion, are more memorable. Jerome Bruner, a cognitive psychologist, suggests that a fact wrapped in a story is 22 times more memorable.

So why do PowerPoint junkies spend all that time putting together their deck of 50 slides? Simple. They wrongly believe that if they "educate" their audience members, they will logically accept the recommendation/solution/product. Facts and figures alone are cold and impersonal and are more likely to elicit a yawn than a yes.

For thousands of years, we have been telling stories as a way of persuading people to do what is in their best interest, and in some cases for dishonest outcomes (Mr. Ponzi comes to mind). I'll bet your parents told you many stories about specific children not listening, resulting in some horribly punitive circumstances.

Good storytelling is hard and takes lots of research and practice. On top of the effort, you'll need to get by the prejudice that "intelligent" people have against using stories as a juvenile form of expression. Neuroscience put this notion to rest years ago, and I've seen the best and the brightest grasp facts and concepts much quicker and thoroughly when put in context and adeptly delivered with nuanced emotion.

So the simple rule for a good story: Make it about a specific person or organization, doing specific things (facts), and then show the effect (emotion) on the outcome relating to your suggestion.

So let's get to work.

> "Be willing to remain silent and recognize the wisdom in silence, rather than to respond critically toward others, events or ideas."
> —Dad, Christmas 2012

Quiet Appreciation

Several years ago, I was at an elementary school in a remote part of Kenya that my sisters were instrumental in raising funds to build. There were about 200 children attending this school, most of whom were from the storied Maasai tribe of East Africa. The Maasai have traditionally pursued a noble pastoral lifestyle as shepherds roaming between Kenya and Tanzania. Their lifestyle has become threatened as their grazing land has become privatized, and generations of shepherds now need to learn a new way of life.

During a school recess, I noticed a young boy about 10 sitting alone on the edge of the grounds. I approached him and asked what he was doing. His answer surprised me at first, but since that time I have come to appreciate the wisdom of his insight, particularly as it pertains to business. His answer to my inquiry: "I'm enjoying the silence."

It seems we have lost the ability to enjoy the silence and in many ways feel threatened by it. Technology intended to increase our effectiveness in business has rather increased our busyness, resulting in high levels of stress. When we lose the ability to appreciate silence, we disconnect ourselves from contemplative thought leading to self-knowledge. Unfortunately, I observe people in business who are so fearful of silence they fill the void with self-destructive and career-ending verbal or written lunacy.

The Trappist monk Thomas Merton wrote that the stress and anxiety created by the lack of contemplative thought was a form of internal human violence. In business, controlling our emotions through silence and thoughtfulness becomes the hallmark of servant leadership. I've seen my share of businesspeople who have to get in the last word and are completely oblivious, or indifferent, to the isolating and damaging impact of this behavior.

It's never been easier to be caught up in the flywheel of communication chaos. Everywhere you turn there is some information provider through your smartphone, television, computer or watch that is trying to break into your mind and set up camp. Contemplative thought used to occur when there was nothing else to do. Those days are gone. Contemplative thought in business and in life needs to be an active and determined choice, or it will not happen. In many ways the best way to connect with people is to first disconnect.

It's funny where we find wisdom when we keep an open mind. For me, it was a 10-year-old shepherd boy half a world away.

So let's get to work.

> "Independence is often misunderstood to mean the ability to 'do what you want,' when in actuality, it is the responsibility to 'do what you ought.'"
> —Dad, Christmas 2007

Character Features

August 2015 marked the 20th anniversary of the death of legendary musician and cultural icon to many Jerry Garcia, lead guitarist and vocalist of the Grateful Dead. The band he founded played its final show in Chicago, marking 50 years of performing.

The music industry is big business, with the well-crafted and scripted personalities of the latest pop or country star yearning to be thrust on the inextinguishable thirst of adoring fans. In a world of biggie-size egos and 24/7 media attention to the lifestyle of the rich and famous, Garcia was an anomaly. His understated creative success in writing and playing music came with a companion: self-destruction through drug addiction, leading to an early death at 53.

I have found in business that it is not uncommon for entrepreneurs with remarkable creative abilities to conceive and build highly successful businesses while having tremendous flaws in their character that eventually lead to their undoing—including the potential subversion of their efforts or a self-imposed solitary existence. I remember speaking to a business associate about this observation, and she remarked that "some people are overbuilt for this world."

Though I don't condone the destructive behaviors of the exceptionally gifted, I've come to accept, without malice, the authenticity of their character. The highest performers in any business enterprise typically come with a few quirks in their personality. They generally surround themselves with sycophants that can create an eerie sense of normalcy. In many ways, the quirks are the seeds of great business success that can't be replicated, leading to the diminution or sale of the business after the founder is gone.

There is a cottage industry of leadership consultants and life coaches that claims the ability to distill the genius of the entrepreneur and institutionalize its essence into the culture of the company. Though it's a noble goal, I've rarely seen it accomplished. The force of personality and uncanny insights associated with gifted entrepreneurs are not easily exported into their management teams or their successor.

If you happen to work for, or with, a gifted though quirky entrepreneur, curtail your instinct to judge and focus on finding the good. I have found their business instincts can be invaluable in looking at your own business.

Apple founder Steve Jobs is a good example of the gifted entrepreneur with a difficult personality. One thing Jobs was fond of saying was "Think Different"—sound advice.

So let's get to work.

> "I'm blessed to have a wonderful collection of family and friends, and living a fulfilled life is much more rewarding when you can share it with others."
> —Adrian, Christmas 2016 (24)

Charlie and Al

For more than 15 years, I've written and received from my son a Christmas letter. They are a cherished gift and tell a beautiful story from innocence to well-grounded maturity. This year, I told him a story of friends Charlie and Al, who met in a small town, each raising large families. Charlie's work required that he move to other locations as far away as California, but their friendship stayed intact. For six decades, they maintained their friendship, and from time to time with their spouses would get together and go on an adventure. They shared many interests and were both galvanized by the curiosity life offered.

After a long—and at the end, difficult—life, Al died. Charlie returned to the small town where they first met to attend Al's funeral and burial. Charlie was the last to leave the cemetery that warm August day, as he wanted to see that Al's casket was properly laid to rest and covered with dirt.

At a small gathering that afternoon, friends and family shared memories of Al, and Charlie was asked to share his thoughts. Charlie pulled from his pocket two documents; the first he read was a letter Al had sent him 25 years earlier. It spoke about some life challenges and ended with a reflection on the importance of meaningful and enduring relationships. Charlie said he kept the letter, knowing someday he would share it, allowing others to know his friend as he did.

Al and Charlie shared a love of poetry and appreciated how a poem can deliver meaning beyond the words themselves. The second document was the poem, "A Friend," written by Eddie Guest, a writer for the Detroit Free Press in the first half of the last century known as the "people's poet." Charlie recited it.

> *A friend is one who stands to share*
>
> *Your every touch of grief and care.*
>
> *He comes by chance, but stays by choice;*
>
> *Your praises he is quick to voice.*

No grievous fault or passing whim
Can make an enemy of him.
And though your need be great or small,
His strength is yours throughout it all.

No matter where your path may turn
Your welfare is his chief concern.
No matter what your dream may be
He prays your triumph soon to see.

There is no wish your tongue can tell
But what it is your friend's as well.
The life of him who has a friend
Is double-guarded to the end.

As you may have suspected, Al was my father and Charlie his friend to the end. Never overlook one of life's greatest gifts: friendship.

> "I asked that this watch remind you of all who came before us and serve as a reminder of your commitment to service and duty to your faith, family and community."
>
> —Dad, Christmas 2007

A Legacy of Unity

Several years ago, I was honored to speak at my hometown Memorial Day celebration in Avon. This is a great privilege, to speak for those who have served our country—some giving what Abraham Lincoln called the "last full measure of devotion."

A tradition of the celebration is the reciting of Lincoln's Gettysburg Address.

Our nation had not yet begun to celebrate Memorial Day when Lincoln delivered his remarks; it wasn't until after the Civil War that we began this annual day of remembrance first known as Decoration Day. There are many interesting connections between Lincoln's words and Memorial Day that have particular meaning today.

Lincoln was honoring the war dead and dedicating a cemetery, but he was doing much more.

He was urging the country to be dedicated to the unfinished work—as he called it, "the great task remaining before us." He was talking about the preservation of our form of government "of the people, by the people, for the people."

Lincoln expressed his determination that the nation remain united, that we remain a single nation, forever one and inseparable.

In many ways we are still a nation trying to live up to the vision in which it was conceived, the concept of a unified people, together dedicated to the proposition that all people are created equal.

I believe that's a thought worth noting and reflecting on as we move through this highly charged and contentious year of political campaigning.

In 1963, 100 years after Gettysburg, Dr. Martin Luther King Jr. stood on the steps of the Lincoln Memorial and delivered his famous "I Have a Dream" speech. King spoke of his vision of "a symphony of brotherhood," standing up for freedom and equality together.

On Memorial Day that year, Vice President Lyndon Johnson spoke in Gettysburg, saying: "The voice of responsible Americans—the voice of those who died here and the great man who spoke here—their voices say, 'Together.' There is no other way."

In Lincoln's first inaugural address, he said:

"The mystic chords of memory, stretching from every battlefield and patriot grave, to every living heart and hearthstone, all over this broad land, will yet swell the chorus of the Union, when again touched, as surely they will be, by the better angels of our nature."

Today, if we listen carefully, we can still hear the better angels of our nature reminding us of the importance of unity. Especially in an election year, it is our responsibility to respect the promise of our nation as one people, together dedicated to our founding ideals.

This Memorial Day, I can think of no better way to honor the men and women who have so nobly fought and died to defend our freedoms than to recall that their service was for each one of us and for all of us together.

> "Commit to excellence in every undertaking and relationship, and I am confident of tremendous success and fulfillment for you."
> —Dad, Christmas 2007

Seven Keys

Spring is my favorite season, as it brings with it a fresh breeze of optimism. It is also a time for college commencements, with an army of new college graduates entering the business world. This spring, I gave a talk at the Saunders School of Business at RIT about what I believed were some of the more important things for them to remember as they worked their way through school and life. Much of what I told them is in my first book, where I dispense what I've learned and observed through my life—or as I like to refer to it, my life's owner's manual.

Subsequent to my talk at Saunders, I was contacted and asked a question I hadn't considered. The student asked my thoughts on the most underrated keys to success. I said that first, I'm not sure how you define success—and maybe that is a discussion we should have—but I'll give you my seven underrated keys to success:

1. **Small details matter.** Far too many try to find a shortcut to business or personal success at the expense of neglecting the little things. Legendary UCLA basketball coach John Wooden told his players: "It's the little details that are vital. Little details make big things happen."

2. **Keep things simple.** Don't overengineer a solution to a problem or the use of a product. The simplest solution is probably the correct one. Apple is the most valuable company in America because it has made its products simple to use.

3. **Prepare and stick to a to-do list every day.** Ivy Lee gave this advice to Charles Schwab, head of Bethlehem Steel in the early 20th century, for which he was paid the equivalent of $300,000 today.

4. **Do the right thing.** Do what is right, not expedient.

5. **Be a good finder in people.** Respect those you meet, and assist them when you can.

6. **Keep an open mind.** Don't be so assured of your point of view that you stop considering others.

7. **Keep moving.** No matter what happens, keep moving forward with optimism, enthusiasm, and the determination to succeed.

As I told the young minds at the Saunders School, it's far more important to achieve excellence in being, rather than excellence in merely achieving.

So let's get to work.

"I believe that now is the time that you can no longer guide me, and I must take responsibility for myself and control my own future."

—Adrian, Christmas 2008 (16)